What's for lunch?

Bread

© 1999 Franklin Watts
96 Leonard Street
London
EC2A 4XD

Franklin Watts Australia
14 Mars Road
Lane Cove
NSW 2066

ISBN 0 7496 3335 2

Dewey Decimal Classification Number 664

A CIP Catalogue record for this book is available from
the British Library

Editor: Samantha Armstrong
Series Designer: Kirstie Billingham
Designer: Jason Anscomb
Consultants: The Federation of Bakers; Flour Advisory Bureau
Reading Consultant: Prue Goodwin, Reading and Language
Information Centre, Reading.

Printed in Hong Kong

What's for lunch?

Bread

Claire Llewellyn

W
FRANKLIN WATTS
NEW YORK • LONDON • SYDNEY

Today we are having bread for lunch.
Bread is full of **fibre**, **protein**,
minerals and **vitamins**.
Eating bread gives us **energy**.

Bread is made mainly from **flour**. Most of the bread we eat is made from wheat flour. Wheat is grown all over the world.

6

Farmers plant wheat seeds in rows
in large fields. They spray the wheat
to protect it against insects and **diseases**.

The young wheat plants grow green leaves
and a tall stem. At the top of each stem
is an **ear.** Tiny flowers grow on the ear.
Later these flowers turn into **grains.**
It is the grains that are used to make flour.

Sometimes bread
is made in a special
shape, such as
this wheatsheaf,
to celebrate a festival.

The fields of wheat change colour and become golden. The grains harden and ripen in the sun and are soon ready to **harvest**. **Combine harvesters** cut the wheat and separate the grain from the stems.
The grain is poured into waiting trailers.

Farmers check the grain is dry and ready for storing. It is then kept in huge containers called **silos.** Some grain is saved for next year's seed. The grain that will be made into bread is sold to **flour millers.**

At the flour mill, the grains are crushed by rollers and then **sifted** into a very fine flour. The miller adds vitamins and minerals to the flour. Flour can be white, brown or **wholemeal.** Different kinds of flour make different types of bread. The flour is now ready to be sold to make bread.

Other **ingredients** are needed to make bread.
These are water, salt and **yeast.**
They are mixed with the flour until it makes
a stretchy **dough.**
Then the dough is mixed or **kneaded.**
The yeast makes the dough **rise.**

yeast

The dough is divided into loaf shapes or else put into tins. Then it is left to rise.

After an hour the dough is twice its original size. This is called **proving.**

The loaves are now ready to be baked in a huge oven.

After about twenty minutes, the loaves of bread are taken out of the oven and turned out of their tins. The bread cools down as it goes along a conveyor belt.

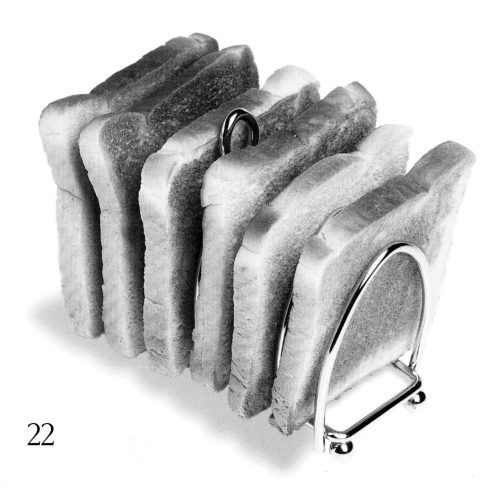

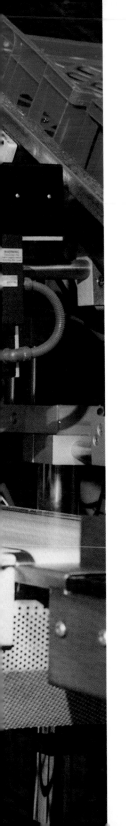

Most of the bread we eat is sliced and packed into plastic bags. Wrapping the bread helps to keep it fresh. It is then taken to shops and supermarkets to be sold.

Different types of bread are eaten all over the world. Bagels are chewy and doughnut-shaped. Pitta bread is flat.

Ciabatta has olive oil added to it and challah has eggs in it. Croissants are sweet and buttery.

Bread is delicious when it is still warm
from the oven.

It is a food that we eat every day.
It is filling, tasty and good for us.

Glossary

combine harvester machine that harvests wheat and separates the grains from the stalks

disease something that attacks plants or animals

dough the bread mixture before it is baked

ear of wheat the top part of the stalk where the grains grow

energy the strength to work and play

fibre something found in some foods which helps us to digest what we eat

flour the fine powder made from crushed wheat grains and which we use to make bread

flour millers people who make flour

grains the seeds of the wheat plant

to harvest to gather in the crop

ingredients the different parts needed to make a dish

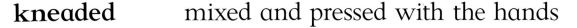

kneaded	mixed and pressed with the hands
minerals	materials found in rocks and also in our food. Minerals help us to stay healthy
protein	something found in food that builds our bodies
proving	leaving the dough so that it can rise
to rise	when the dough puffs up because of the yeast and becomes light and airy
sifted	when something is put through a sieve to make it fine and powdery
silos	huge storage containers for grain
vitamin	something found in food which keep us healthy
wholemeal	flour made with all of the crushed wheat grain
yeast	something added to bread dough to make it rise

Index

Picture credits: Holt Studios International: 6-7 (Willem Harinck), 8 (Nigel Cattlin), 10, 13 (Inga Spence),
15 (Willem Harinck); Flour Advisory Bureau: 16; Holt Studios International: 19 (Nigel Cattlin); Federation of Bakers 20, 23,
24 (Tony Ross); Steve Shott: cover, backcover;
All other photographs Tim Ridley, Wells Street Studios, London.
With thanks to Charlotte Trundley, Nyran Sri-Pathmanathan and Alex Wright.